JACKPOT!

The Step-by-Step Guide

To A Winning

On-Campus Recruitment Campaign

JACKPOT!

A Step-by-Step Guide

To A Winning

On-Campus

Recruitment Campaign

~

James C. Allison

TALENTLINK BUSINESS LIBRARY

Trafford Publishing

Editing & Layout: Allison Philpot

Graphic Design: Chris Cole

Printed in Victoria, BC, Canada.

ISBN: 978-1-4269-1523-9

*Our mission is to efficiently provide the world's finest, most comprehensive book publishing
service, enabling every author to experience success. To find out how to publish your
book, your way, and have it available worldwide, visit us online at www.trafford.com*

Trafford rev. 9/28/2009

 www.trafford.com

North America & international
toll-free: 1 888 232 4444 (USA & Canada)
phone: 250 383 6864 ♦ fax: 812 355 4082

Feedback about JACKPOT!

"This straightforward and complete guide to recruiting doesn't miss a trick! It will start you evaluating your recruiting techniques and immediately add value to your process. Just when you think everything is covered, you get more tips and guidance to successful recruiting"

Tim Mulder
CFO/Senior Vice President
Davidson's Inc.

"This book is a must have for any organization looking to strengthen their talent base. JACKPOT is a precise how-to guide on Campus recruiting."

Paul Perrier
Director of Operations
Wal-Mart Canada

"With so many HR reference books, sometimes it's difficult to differentiate one from the other. This one is a 'must have book' and it belongs in every HR professional's library."

Susy Snopek
Human Resources
Savage Arms

"You will definitely hit the JACKPOT reading this! A creative, must-have resource and thorough "step by step" guide with essential tools to assist you in understanding your target market first off; branding your company and then attracting and retaining the best talent through this creative campaign to ensure success. Why do it any other way? This is definitely in my toolkit".

Genevieve Martin
Corporate Recruiter
Shoppers Drug Mart

"Jamie Allison is a HR visionary with the ability to take a strategic vision and create the functional change to implement it. Jamie is strong at recognizing people's strength and fostering a model to allow them to maximize their potential."

Kevin Kirkpatrick
President
Avery Professional Group

TALENTLINK

Most TalentLink Library Publications and materials are available at special quantity discounts for bulk purchases. Special excerpts and articles can be created to fit specific needs.

For Details email:

talentlinkpublishing@rogers.ca

Table of Contents

Acknowledgments

I am truly excited to share this book with you and I hope that it provides you with tools and ideas that you can use in your business. When developing a guide like this, one quickly realizes the importance of a strong team and a network of coaches to bring it to fruition. I have been lucky in my career to have met and learned from so many inspirational people. Some jump out in my mind right away, such as the late Peter Urs Bender, whose inspirational story and incredible ability to make people feel they can do anything motivated me to pursue this endeavour. Peter passed away while I was writing this book, but even while he was battling for his life he offered encouraging words and coaching. He will be truly missed by so many, but his legacy lives on in all of those he touched with his works and inspirational personality.

When thinking about whom to thank I am reminded of the kind words and coaching I received from past and current Human Resources colleagues and bosses. These include Chuck Farrell, Chris Roshko, Irene Rumak, Heather Sheehan, Marilyn Jackson, Bob Noftal, and of course my entire HR teams at Peterborough Regional Health Centre and Wal-Mart/SAM's who inspire me everyday with their own dedication and skills. I am so lucky to have worked with each and every one of these people.

I have also been influenced by many business people from various industries, professions and experiences, who have each opened my mind to new ideas and ways of looking at the world. My very first marketing meeting at Cadbury Chocolate, for instance, taught me the importance of preparation, and that design makes a difference in every aspect of business, and these lessons I carry with me still. I must also acknowledge the influence of Ken Crema of Electronic Direct Marketing, Teletech Canada and since then MCCI. Ken epitomizes a focus on personal business success. He is one of those guys that can sell anything to anyone.

These people and these lessons have taught me to look at a gamut of situations with a broad sense and a critical business eye, and for these skills I am eternally grateful.

Of course the biggest influence on my life is my family. Heartfelt thanks go out to my wife, Marsi, for supporting me when I am irrational and for making me feel like I am truly invaluable. Thanks as well to the princesses in my life – Alexa and Olivia, who make my life complete. *Girls: You know our promise!* Thanks as well to my parents and brother for believing that I can do anything.

Special Thanks to: Chris Cole for her fabulous graphics work, Allison Philpot for making my writing presentable, Alan Simmons for convening the political round table and keeping the ducks away, Lynda for lending her support on this project (even during Superbowl), Dave for being one of the two funny accountants I know, and Tim for being the other.

Thanks again to Peter Urs Bender. He signed a book for me as follows:

Jamie:

"I have never met an HR professional like you. I have never been much for HR guys (they never get why marketing is

so important), but you have changed my mind. You make a difference."

Peter

It is amazing what a compliment can do, Peter.

Rest in Peace friend.

Introduction

There are many books "out there" that describe the impending demographic crunch, the current talent shortage (even during up and down economic times) and the importance of effective campus recruitment. However, I have come across very few that give a step-by-step approach to putting together an effective on-campus campaign. Many organizations realize they need a presence on campus, and will benefit from incorporating students into their organizations, but few companies have the "toolkit" to make it happen and to take full advantage of the opportunities available to them.

The aim of this guide is to change that. Yours may be a small firm that needs to put a few, low-cost tricks in place to level the playing ground and play to your competitive advantage. Or perhaps yours is a large company looking to develop a cohesive plan, get everyone focusing on key goals. Whatever your situation, you will be able to find ideas here to help. The techniques and tools that I have outlined and designed for this book have come from years of recruitment experience, both on and off-campus, in a number of highly competitive industries. Not all of the steps are for all companies or situations, but it will provide you with some new ideas, helpful action lists and some tools to help you develop a successful campaign.

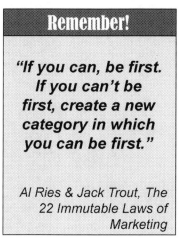

Remember!

"If you can, be first. If you can't be first, create a new category in which you can be first."

Al Ries & Jack Trout, The 22 Immutable Laws of Marketing

The truth about a campus presence is this: it doesn't matter if you are a small business or a Fortune 500 company, a campus presence can be a competitive advantage for you if you work it right. There are new, innovative methods of sourcing people that are being implemented everyday. Watch for them and learn. Use these methods, and what you learn in this book, as a base to build your campaign.

This is a competition where you can be on the winning side!

Chapter One

THE CHANGING WORKFORCE

Aging Population

In the 1990s the term "War For Talent" was coined, and with it came a massive change in how organizational search techniques developed, and how candidates made employment decisions. We learned from "The Bubble" that occurred in high tech: unprecedented competition for talent resulted in offers of inflated compensation, stock options and exaggerated job titles. When that Internet Bubble "popped," so did much of the investment in North America's Talent Pool. Sourcing focus dropped and campus hiring took a negative hit. That trend is happening again with the current down cycle.

However, even now that downward trend is beginning to Reverse. Current metrics are moving into positive territory. In September of 2009, David Aplin Recruiting reported that 75 percent of surveyed Canadian firms expressed optimism that Canadian employment rates will improve or stabilize for the remainder of the year. According to the results of an employer survey published by Michigan State University managers had expected to increase hiring in 2006 by 20% for associate, bachelor and master degree graduates. As well, Canada started the year off in 2007 with the lowest unemployment rate in years. The current downturn has put a dent in those statistics, but in North America and across the globe, markets in healthcare, technology and specialized positions are showing signs of heating up. Companies that are not prepared to deal with this reality will be left behind with drastic consequences. The time is returning when a lack of organizational talent can be the difference between business success and bankruptcy.

Widespread thinking regarding the job market of the future is that the need for skilled professionals will once again become very acute. This time, in addition to a booming technology driver and a lack of graduates, which coloured the landscape of recent past, the same generational swing that has slowly been changing our political climates and economies will have a dramatic effect on the workforce. You may be sick of hearing about the pressure that "Baby Boomers" put on our system, but the reality is that this pressure is realized in so many studies that it would be foolhardy to dismiss it.

When I co-hosted an economic talk show in the mid-90s, even then prognosticators were looking at the effect of Baby Boomers on our jobs, real estate and stock markets. With my financial planner partner Dan Seabrooke, I interviewed David Cork, a financial analysis and author of *The Pig and the Python*. In that interview David said:

"The Boomers will change the face of the economy. This group has dictated housing markets, politics and the overall economy. It shouldn't be a surprise when cottages become the 'hot property to have in the next couple of decades'."

David was echoing the thoughts of other demographers like David Foot, author of *Boom Bust and Echo*. Foot also made the case that the demographic trend will change the economy, and those that anticipate the impact can profit from the changes, while those who miss it will suffer.

Empirical demographic data is still backing what David Foot and David Cork have said. Admittedly, things like technology, outsourcing/offshoring and business efficiencies have tempered the massive impact of Baby Boomers predicted in the late 90s. However, the gap between jobs and available workers left behind when the boomers leave the scene will undeniably be too large to ignore. Efforts within your business today and in the next few years must prepare for this. Companies that prepare now and position themselves positively will be the ones that win as the country – the world! – eases into this inevitable "gap."

Student Hiring Trends

As mentioned earlier, projections for student hiring are already beginning to trend upward again, signaling a need for preparation and planning on the part of potential employers. CollegeGrad.com reported that 2006 hiring levels for new grads were projected to be 7.8% higher than 2005 levels. The current blip in hiring will ultimately turn in the near future and cause additional pressure due to lack of activity on campus. That same website is also predicting a combination of greater need for skilled workers, a stronger economy (in Canada in particular), and preparation for succession planning as considerable factors influencing companies that are working to put in place aggressive on-campus plans.

If you haven't begun to design your campus presence for your company, now is definitely the time to begin.

Generational Mix & Generation "Y"

In order to be successful in the development of your plan, you have to understand your target market or markets. There are very specific ways of identifying market characteristics, and these will be discussed in a later section. But to begin, it is important to have a broad understanding of the demographics of your target group, and common behaviours of the campus audience.

A mistake often made is to assume that the current group of campus hires will be just like we were when we were in their shoes. I am sure that most of us can think of a time when we have heard a seasoned manager say "they should just be happy to have a job," or ask why a value proposition is being tailored to this group because "we are choosing them, and they would be lucky to get this opportunity." Sure, in some markets that is true – but it is precisely that attitude that will kill a campus campaign during times of high competition. As well, the generation being recruited right now holds a very different values-system than do generations in the current workplace. This is important to keep in mind.

Remember – you can't assume that you know your targets. You just can't. You know the old saying about what happens when you ASSUME don't you? If you don't – ask around. Someone can and will let you know!

Do the Research!

Bruce Tulgan of *Rainmaker Thinking* has done some amazing research regarding generations in the workforce, and Generation Y in particular. *Rainmaker Thinking* breaks down the multi-generational workforce into a number of groups. Generation X (born 1965 – 1977) and Generation Y (born 1977-1989) now make up over half of the current workforce, according to recent studies by Tulgan's group, Generation Y is the fastest growing segment of the workforce. Tulgan has concluded that this group of workers has high expectations for their careers and the workplace, and that they have a strong affinity for volunteerism. That is great news for people in the healthcare and service fields, so long as they find effective ways to capitalize on it.

In a healthcare organization I was once involved with, we surveyed engagement levels among staff. We found that one of the key motivations for employee engagement was the feeling that they were doing something that gave back to the community, and that their roles and workplaces added value to the lives of other people. If that is an incentive, an impetus for people, then what better time and place to capitalize on it than when Generation Y is entering the workforce?

When thinking about your campus presence and the recruitment of young workers, you should also be strongly considering the expectation of this newest generation around technology. They like quick responses and need to be engaged. Technology is a good tool, yes, but personalizing with a "high touch" approach is what gives organizations a competitive advantage with this group. They like engaging people. They like to be in teams and they like to learn from other talented colleagues.

Campuses now represent members of all of generational groups, but the majority of new hires will inevitably come from the Generation Y age group. So get to know what these people want in a job, and begin to create a value proposition for them

The following is a list of key characteristics that *Rainmaker Thinking* has outlined for Generation Y. As mentioned, this group now makes up the majority of today's campus population.

Generation Y members are:

1. **Highly self confident and upbeat**

2. **The most education-minded in history**

3. **Paving the way to a more open and tolerant society**

4. **Leading a new wave of volunteerism** (This is reinforced by jurisdictional requirements for

service-related co-ops at the high school level, such as within the province of Ontario.)

(Source: RainmakerThinking.com)

Where the buzz in recent years has been about a free agent market and decreased organizational loyalty when speaking of Generation X, the current campus group may be changing that thinking slightly. Brainstorm Consulting, a British Columbia-based campus recruitment consulting and research organization, recently found in one of their studies that 62% of decided students would like to find an organization where they could spend their whole career. That means that the organization that can present development opportunities and exhibit great work teams can quite possibly reduce turnover, increase employee loyalty and produce higher results.

What an opportunity to meet human resources goals in the coming years through effective campus recruiting!

The "Experienced" Student

Although we tend to focus on the "traditional student" when we talk about college recruiting, the landscape of college demographics has changed considerably in recent years. With a focus on e-learning, "twilight" classes and other flexibility initiatives, the student you may be looking for could have more (and more varied) work experience than your recruiters.

The prevalence of career switching, late career job changes, re-training and upgrading have made post-secondary and advanced education much more accessible and more common for the work-experienced individual. These changes create marketing challenges for the recruiting organization, but the potential opportunities in this circumstance can be substantial.

Diversify your Pipeline!

With the work-experienced student, you have the opportunity to hire a workforce veteran, someone who comes with skills and knowledge. This experience base may have come from a different industry or a different work culture, but it can be very valuable when you are looking at "flattening" the learning curve for a new hire.

Often, experienced students are very focused on what they want out of their education and their next job. They have already passed the "college drinking years" and are focused on creating the life they want from a realistic viewpoint. They may have lost some of the "rose-coloured glasses" frequently found in more youthful students, but often make up for it with pragmatic expectations and a drive to achieve.

Your recruitment efforts in addressing the needs of the experienced student must be different from what you would provide to the "traditional" student. Special attention must be paid to the intricacies of the lives of these people. Think of their schedules, for instance. They may be at school during nights and only on campus at that time (they are there to work and would prefer to be home with their families). They must see value in what they are offered from recruiting efforts. If you are planning an event, for example, plan it out in a structured way that addresses their needs, such as offering it during off-hours. Be sure you fit into their plans, because you can be sure that they have them.

Targeting experienced students, even if it means more work, can be beneficial for another reason. Many of these individuals that have home commitments and have had to make heavy sacrifices that impact their families or livelihood in order to return to school can be extremely committed to the organization they choose to join afterwards. When I worked at Teletech in the late 1990s, I hired a gentleman named Lawrence. Lawrence had been out of work and had re-trained through a computer program as technical support. I was hiring for a major internet service provider at the time, and Lawrence's skill-base was not as full as some of the less experienced, younger staff. However, it was obvious that Lawrence had a drive to do well in his new field. He joined the organization, and it grew exponentially – from 200 workers to over a thousand in a year, during Lawrence's early time with us.

As things go, my contact with Lawrence was limited as he got into his job. But what I will always remember is what happened at Christmas of that first year. I received a Christmas card from Lawrence in my mail. Inside was a note from his family to mine. It said: "Jamie: Thank you for giving me the greatest gift I could have received, my job at Teletech. I will always appreciate it. Lawrence"

It is easy to forget the impact that a recruiter (or anyone for that matter) can have when it works for everyone. Dedication: Lawrence, the experienced student, had it in boatloads. You don't want to miss that boat! As mandatory retirement phases out to offset the talent gap, your presence in the market for experienced students will become more and more important.

Summary

With the right management, each generation within your company will add to what could become a very complementary team. When you are designing an on-campus presence, remember that you have more than one audience. The same broad recruiting principles apply across the board, but be sure to take into consideration the diversity between audiences. Just as you would not focus on one campus or one cultural background exclusively, your efforts should not focus on one age group. Companies that succeed will be those that capitalize on each core group to meld a team of diverse talent.

Similarly, be sure to examine what it is your target market wants in a *job*. Research it, talk to your newest employees, ask questions and listen to the answers in an unbiased fashion. The reasons that you joined your company or chose your field of expertise may be completely different from the reasons your target market are considering the same field. Define the target, and use the techniques in the rest of this book to benefit from engaging that group with success.

Chapter Two

THE EMPLOYMENT BRAND

Branding: What is it?

One of the most popular business 'buzz words' of recent times is **Branding**. I admit it – I am a strong proponent of this concept and am pleased to see it play an increasingly important role in the way Human Resources programs do business.

Traditionally, branding applied only to products like *Tide* and *Caramilk*. Now it means so much more: companies can be a brand; programs can be a brand; heck, even we, ourselves, can be a brand!

For some people, this growth in branding is seen as a daunting concept, especially for those that haven't grabbed onto the idea at work. An organization may have a poor brand in the marketplace, have no real brand in its target market, or may not be aware of its market perception or reputation. The fact is that opportunities are plentiful if branding is allowed to flourish. My advice is this: Make a brand plan. Talk to a marketer. You won't regret it!

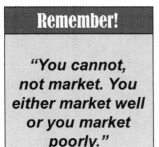

Remember!

"You cannot, not market. You either market well or you market poorly."
Peter Urs Bender

I mentioned earlier that Peter Urs Bender has been a real inspiration to me. He took great pains in building his brand as a speaker and management consultant. I clearly remember the first experience I had with Peter: I had heard about his keynotes and I was organizing a learning event for staff. I found his information on a website and sent an e-mail to him requesting more information. That same day I received a personal voicemail that thanked me for my interest and suggested a one-on-one discussion. Less than two days later I received copies of two of his books, autographed and with a special note thanking me for being in discussions, along with his cell phone number to call if I had more questions.

Of course that positively swayed my decision to hire Peter for my event. Peter was an awesome speaker, so I did not regret it (he delivered his brand promise!), but it was his efforts that opened the door wide, and handed him his opportunity. Peter literally *managed* my perception of his personal brand in a very positive way.

What do you think – Can the same impact take place with personal notes to a student, a small token or a card? **You bet it can! Personalize where you can!** A strong employment brand can mean the difference between wasted effort and a sustainable campus recruitment campaign.

When it comes to branding, we all know organizations that do a good job of it – think of Coke, Wal-Mart, Nike, Baptiste Health, Microsoft. There are many ways that those organizations (and yours!) benefit from strong branding – consider these below.

Become a Magnet

A strong brand "pulls" employees to an organization. Branding is a cheap, and ultimately effective, way for an organization to turn the tables from seeking, to receiving applicants. Some organizations have a strong enough reputation through methodical branding practices that potential candidates feel honoured when approached or recruited by one of these organizations. The perception is that the "best" (often determined through carefully managed reputation-building practices) seek the best talent.

Target Your Search

By clearly identifying what it represents and looks for in employees, an organization can attract key target candidates; unqualified or inappropriate candidates will "self-select" themselves out of the process. A sustained, targeted program can reach key markets in a cost effective manner, and can find as a reward, very positive results.

Level the Playing Field

Regardless of the size of an organization, a clearly articulated and appealing brand can actually provide success at the same levels of much larger or more affluent organizations. This is an easy way to create a competitive advantage – and a level playing field for smaller players.

More Resumes, Qualified Applicants & Faster Recruitment

As more people are drawn to an organization, the more internal processes benefit from an increase in qualified candidates. This means it is easier to get the right person, in a much faster process, through a shorter recruitment cycle.

Sense of Engagement

Employee engagement can drive positive company results. Branding is important in this way, as it can enhance engagement by defining a proper fit for both the organization and potential employees. In the long run, branding can also lead to improved selection processes, internal people-practices, and employee retention.

Earn The Right

When top candidates are consistently drawn to an organization, that business "earns the right" to be more and more selective during hiring. They have, in essence, earned the reputation of an *employer of choice*. Arthur Soler, a former CEO of Cadbury Trebor Allan (CTAI), used Proctor & Gamble as an example when he said "they have earned the right" to put candidates through one of the most rigorous student recruitment processes he knew of by consistently working to be the employer of choice for marketing students.

Suggested Reading

Secrets Of Power Marketing
Peter Urs Bender & George Torok
THE ACHIEVEMENT GROUP
May 1999

The Brand You50
(Reinventing Work)
Tom Peters
Alfred A. Knopf September 1999

So, it is easy to recognize that there is value in becoming a strong employment brand and an elite organization. However, the big question is how you get there. To begin, you need to treat it like a journey, step by step. Start your process at the beginning by identifying where you are today with your brand. Honestly acknowledge that as your starting point. Next you plan the route and execute – this guide will help you do that.

Where is Your Brand Now?

In order to promote your brand, or to identify what you want your brand to be, you need to know where your brand is now. There are a number of questions you need to ask, and the answers you collect must be candid.

The process of developing a brand needs to involve a marketing department (if the organization is big enough to have one), employees, and focus groups of the target market. Regardless of the scale of brand development project to be undertaken, the questions are the same, and need to be answered before building a path for others to follow. History will help you plan, so the questions must be answered as accurately as possible.

Step 1: Questions to Jumpstart Branding and the Development of A Brand Message

1. What is our current Brand internally (staff) and externally (with our target market)? How are we perceived?

2. What in our work culture or work design makes us a unique place to work (or at least what do target candidates think?)? What makes us different from our competitors? What are the features and benefits of working with us, above and beyond the competitors?

3. How do we stack up against our major competitors? Are we outpacing them at recruiting top talent? If you ask students or career center reps, who has the best reputation and why? Ask them and yourself what is it we have to do to be number one in our field. If we do "stack up" are we differentiating ourselves from our competitors? Are we followers or leaders?

4. Who are the overall major recruiters/players on campus? Who does a great job and who draws the crowds at events? Hint: Here is where you look outside of your industry. Again, ask your career centre contacts – they can point you in the right direction.

Step 2: Selling Points

The next part of determining where you are now is to look at your selling points. Sales and marketing people always think in terms of features and benefits. What is it that appeals to the buyer (candidate)? What fills a need or want for that person?

By getting an idea what your own features and benefits are, you can begin to build a base to your value proposition and brand messaging. Think beyond the standard pay and benefits information. Think about work-life balance, research possibilities, a career management program. Start by getting it all out there, and later in the process match the candidates to what you offer.

Remember!

"Your premium brand had better be delivering something special, or it's not going to get the business."

Warren Buffett

... or in this case, the candidates!

What are Features & Benefits in the context of employee relationships?

Features: Distinguishing facts about your organization (Best-Practice Procedures, Key Products etc.)

Benefits: Outcomes valued by possible candidates and your target audience, such as: working for the #1 company in the region, work-life balance outcomes for staff, urban living etc.

The following is an exercise that you can do on your own or as part of group (think about using a cross-functional internal recruitment committee for this). The concept may seem simple, but really working through this exercise can break down walls, encourage innovative brainstorming, and promote open thinking that can bring results and brilliant marketing messages.

Features & Benefits discussion meeting:

Issues to ponder:

1. Discuss the definitions of features and benefits with your recruitment committee. Refine these definitions as you need, to make them work for the entire group.

2. Brainstorm about employment benefits and features of your competitors and other organizations.

3. List your own organizations' features and benefits. Allow your list to grow long, and then highlight key selling factors. Which are the most compelling?

4. Prioritize the list you have created, and highlight your top 5 Benefits and Top 5 Features.

5. Keep the list you have created handy as you go forward with your planning – it will be your check and balance as you plan. Always bring the group back to the statements you started with, and ensure that the message you are developing is true to the organizations' features and benefits, and capitalizes on what makes the organization unique. Remember – in order to be competitive, some of your features and benefits may need to be developed!

Features and Benefits worksheet:

Features	Benefits

Step 3: Go! The development of the brand message now centres around the key question:

How can we convey our message concisely,

and engage the hearts and minds

of our target market?

Unless you are a Marketing executive, branding may be a new term for you. One of the best sources of a branding methodology for human resources programs, projects and innovative thinking can be found at TomPeters.com. The guru that brought the business world *In Search of Excellence* has long been a proponent of branding projects and programs. Branding your organization can be as important as the product or service you provide.

> *"Regardless of age, regardless of position, regardless of the business we happen to be in, all of us need to understand the importance of branding. We are CEOs of our own companies: Me Inc. To be in business today, our most important job is to be head marketer for the brand called You."*   *-Tom Peters*

Hit his website, read a presentation, share your thoughts in his Brand Café and take in as many ideas as you can.

Most of all, don't get stuck on your industry. Find gems in other work areas and apply them to your own branding efforts. Always tailor those efforts to suit your situation, but recognize that you aren't working in isolation. Become a brand follower. Read the Peters' books *Project 50*, *The Brand You 50* and

Re-Imagine. At the very least, Peters will energize you and challenge your thinking.

Your brand, if it is marketed correctly, quickly and accurately tells possible candidates who you are, why it is the best place to be, and almost immediately paints a positive, clear message in their mind. At Cadbury, a brand-driven packaged good company, we had a CEO that explained the impact of branding on HR efforts. He emphasized that it is branding that sets up the perception of "best in show" for a company, and likewise it is branding that attracts people to the company. This means less searching efforts within the company itself; suddenly, the company enjoys a magnetism for quality talent, without the bulk of effort to find and hire them.

A great example of a powerful career brand and recruitment innovation is Proctor & Gamble. P&G is a leader in recruitment. In its campus recruitment efforts, it runs a case study for candidates; a rigourous process and a bold step when trying to attract young talent. There are very few organizations that could actually include a step like this in their process, but P&G has built such a great career brand that students and other candidates are drawn to the organization, and are willing to go through extra effort just to work there.

P&G is one example of a great brand, however, we can't all fall in to that type of situation. Your organization may be one that has a poor brand, or no real tangible brand within your target market as yet. Your effort, then, becomes focused upon instigating, revitalizing, or changing your brand. That's okay – there are encouraging examples of this as well.

Consider the branding transformation of the Federal Bureau of Investigation in the United States. The Bureau had a staunch, bureaucratic brand perception to the students they were targeting as future employees. Because of this, the FBI was not having the kind of success they wanted at the campus level. In a bold move, they put their brand development in the hands of the students at their key target campuses. Students were charged with developing a brand for their campus and the results were outstanding.

Remember!

Branding Doesn't Happen Overnight!

A Consistent, Ongoing Approach is Imperative to Reap the Dividends of a Strong Brand.

With the valuable input from the FBI's target market, the organization's brand was revived to tailor to the campus scene. It created a funky, popular presence that capitalized on the mystique of investigative crime fighting, and spy excitement. The FBI recruitment program improved considerably in a short amount of time, due in large part to successful branding of the organization's competitive advantages, and the development of an organizational brand based on feedback from the target market.

Sample Brand-building Tactics: Below are a few nuggets – ideas – for your organization to consider when putting together a branding program. Take them, work them, and use them to build yourself into something unique and attractive to your target market.

➲ Apply for "Top Company" lists. Being listed as a good employer and a "Best Company to Work For" is very beneficial for your overall and on-campus brand. Other lists that match your employment brand ("Best Companies for Families", "Most Admired Corporate Cultures", "Best Cities to Live In" etc.) are also worth the effort. Getting on these lists will support your branding message.

➲ Keep and publish statistics and favourable reviews and/ or articles about your organization's brand-related programs. If you have a work-life balance brand message, for instance, be sure to list users of a company-led exercise program or wellness program.

➲ Evaluate your brand-related programs. Highlight key successful ones, and focus efforts on improvement of the others.

➲ Launch new programs and update existing ones with a focus on design that matches your employment brand.

➲ Sponsor events that match your recruitment brand. For example, run a 5K family run to match your lifestyle branding, or an entrepreneur competition to match your innovation brand.

➲ Ensure that your recruiters know that branding is important, and that they understand how to boost the brand in their efforts. *Recruiter development is essential.*

➲ Actively promote your people practices in Human Resources forums like professional association meetings (like SHRM, HRPAO etc...), conferences and in human resources profession publications.

➲ Use any of the college recruitment campaign tactics outlined in this guide but, always keep your brand message "front-of-mind."

➲ Work with your Marketing and Public Relations departments to send out proactive story ideas and employee profiles that promote and enhance your brand message with media and business magazines.

Chapter Three

PREPARING THE CAMPAIGN

Recruitment Needs Assessment

Before an organization can effectively develop a campus campaign to support its branding, the **corporate recruitment needs** must be determined. Many large organizations have recruitment priority plans, or workforce plans, but even smaller firms can use basic techniques to predict human resource needs.

The business case behind every successful campaign starts with a needs assessment. The further into the future you can plan and forecast needs, the more focused your efforts can be, and the more impressive your successes. Start building your needs assessment by considering a few key issues, outlined below.

Identify vacancy or created vacancy number.

Take a look at the current vacant entry-level positions you have in your organization. Of course, immediate openings always take precedence and that becomes your planning start point. Beyond that number, have departments or Managers in your organizations outline expected entry-level turnover during the planning period of one school year. Some organizations will have a very accurate "guesstimate" due to in-depth analysis of past turnover etc... Smaller organizations will have a more difficult time identifying this number, but this is where I would encourage all organizations to become more pro-active anyway. Consider your needs over multiple years (succession planning), the restriction of labour pools if you anticipate this impacting your industry and the need to develop employees for management roles. For example, a retail organization may commit to hire more Business graduates than they have vacancies for in order to off-set future turnover and their need for high level talent.

Again, make the case in your organization for proactive recruitment. This is a long-term process, but it can easily pay off considering graduation occurs once a year and the student labour pool can experience considerable change before the hiring period occurs again. The further ahead you can plan vacancies, the better your talent pipeline will become.

Consider what it is that defines a successful person for this company, and in this particular job?

When thinking about this question, you will need to consider every job with every specific nuance. Outline a profile of a successful hire for each differing position. The Candidate Profile Form at the end of this book offers a simple format for gauging the definition of a successful incumbent based on behaviours and traits. You can chose the depth to which you delve into this – some companies use test results, succession plans and core competencies outlined in their position descriptions, for instance.

After you determine what you are looking for, ask your current employees why they came to your organization. Ask them what they like about your workplace, and what they like about their teams and fellow employees? This information will give you a realistic picture of what it really means to work in your organization. Two additional positive outcomes of asking these questions of your staff are that you can better match your publicity and employment brand with the reality of your workplace while providing recognition and value to your staff members. People appreciate being asked their opinion about their work and workplaces and this allows you to do that. Employee involvement in this early stage can help the organization move towards its staff becoming the unofficial recruiters of your company.

Examine your expectations.

Are the expectations of your definition of successful employees appropriate to campus recruitment? Are these expectations aimed at a student hire level?

Plan the search.

In planning your search for employees, start the process by defining your targets. Using your sample definition of successful employees, corporate vision and job requirements, identify who it is you really want to recruit. Then use this information to define your own competitive advantage. You can realize that advantage over your competitors by "playing on your strengths". Focus on the few things you do very well and finding the match for that in your candidate pool. Your strength is not in improving your weaknesses (unless they are glaring negatives), but rather using your strengths as a means to set yourself part from competition.

For example, at a healthcare institution I worked at, we tied together our target candidates, job requirements and our campaign limitations, and found that it was better to recruit on campus out of province. Universities outside our province better amplified our competitive advantage, and the competition for a smaller organization in those areas was not as fierce.

One Caution: Be careful not to put all of your eggs in one basket. If you strike out, the entire season's campaign could be wasted. At minimum, the diversity of your talent pool could suffer. Consistently sourcing candidates from a single recruitment source, educational background or experience type can work against the development of successful teams.

Diversity in teams and talents starts with knowing your recruitment audience and from actively looking for a spectrum of individuals that match your requirements.

Determine and Approve a Budget.

A budget should be well understood by every member of your team, and be a contributor to your success. Put a budget together by:

Ha!

"It's clearly a budget. It's got a lot of numbers in it."

George W. Bush

1. Reviewing your Campaign Goals and Objectives

2. Outlining your sources of funds

3. Outlining the campaign costs

4. Drawing up the overall budget

5. Presenting the information and budget for Approval and Mandate

Simple Budget Overview:

Student Recruitment Budget	Implementation August -		June
Item/Cost	Budget	Actual	Variance	Overall
Advertising -brochures - newspaper				
Food				
Travel of Recruiters				
Draw Items				
Photography and Design				
Sponsorships				
Campus ads				
Recruiter time (some orgs count this)				
Printing				
Equipment				
				$$$$$$$

Cost per student hire can be calculated by dividing total costs by the number of hires. Be careful not to artificially inflate the direct cost by allocating all "branding-building" activities to specific hires early in your marketing efforts.

The Recruitment Committee

As a human resources professional, I am always promoting the importance of HR practices in the functioning of a successful business. I make a point to emphasize that HR people can't do it alone – recruitment plans are best when they tap into staff from all areas of the organization. The truth is that in order to find the right message, the right audience and effectively deliver on your value proposition, the building blocks of your campaign must come from key members of your organization.

A great starting point for this work is a recruitment group or committee comprised of those key members of the organization. In addition to any recruiter(s) in the company, this committee should have a broad membership. It should be small enough to get things done (there is nothing worse than a committee that takes four years to plan an annual campaign), yet have the right people at the table.

To build your recruitment committee, I offer my advice: I would suggest the inclusion a member from senior management to ensure corporate buy-in and support where needed, a marketing representative with a keen understanding of your target market, and a few staff members from target departments or professions that are close to, and possibly recent alumni of, the target markets of your campaign. This group can give you the direction and operational expertise to design an incredible campaign.

What does the group do?

The recruitment committee groups acts as your steering committee for the recruitment campaign. Some compose a group targeting only student recruitment, but smaller organizations can apply the principles and plans to overall recruitment. The key is to engage people that want to make a difference, have an interest in creating a top-notch talent stream, and bring credibility to the process.

As many individuals in this group will be coming from areas other than human resources, it is important to give them the professional knowledge and tools to allow them to make good decisions and enable them to make creative solutions work.

Committee Education

The recruitment committee has to gain both an understanding and appreciation of the importance of their role in the long-term development of your organization. Recruitment initiatives must take into account not only organizational fit and culture change, but ultimately the retention of key people in each department. Representatives from recruiting departments who understand this function of the committee will add value to the campaign for the entire organization.

As well, you must provide background information to your committee. This includes:

- ⊃ key recruitment activities to date,

- ⊃ established human resources plans

- ⊃ established marketing materials, and

- ⊃ expectations for the committee and the campaign.

An overview of the recruitment process, including interviewing, competency profiles, and/or any processes applicable to campus plans, should be reviewed.

The "Unwritten, but SHOULD be written rule":

Make it interesting!

Recruitment *is* Marketing... Marketing executives make their presentations interesting. If you have ever been to a formal project launch meeting, or key brainstorming session with those who know what they're doing, you will know what I mean.

Create the excitement! Ask a marketing person for tips, or try at the very least, make your presentation and committee meeting interactive. Transfer your passion for this project to the team, or as Tom Peters says, make it a WOW project.

Ask your committee "What is the WOW factor for you?"

Remember!

To make your project a success, figure out what you are trying to accomplish. It isn't good enough to say: "I want to hire some students."

Duh!
So does every other organization!

If you were writing a business plan it wouldn't end there. Think of this as a business plan.

Smart Goals

Now is the time you need to use your SMART Goals:

* **Specific**

* **Measurable**

* **Achievable**

* **Realistic**

* **Timed**

Throughout this guide I will often refer to setting and re-visiting goals. Always use the SMART principles to set these goals. Using them will take you from a position of defending your projects and budgets, to one of being a positive contributor, to the orchestrator of success for your organization.

Remember – you need to show the CEO that you have a goal, that it is a "stretch goal," and that you can identify when you have reached that goal.

Outcomes are everything.

Target School Determination

Broad campus marketing has changed in recent years, resulting in niche marketing and targeting of schools as most effective techniques. By identifying and determining target schools, an organization, regardless of size, can deepen a relationship within the school, and promote a branded image, capitalizing on that relationship.

Target determination works like this: With your needs assessment data, research which organizations provide the qualified applicants you are looking for. Your recruitment committee can help you define this list, and highlight those with good reputations for graduates. (Remember, they will have bias if they are alumni, and your best target may not actually be the school allocated as number one by the committee. Just a word of warning.)

Often your competitive advantage comes from targeting an untapped school that hasn't yet branded itself. Look to some of the universities in smaller centres, for instance, where the large head offices don't have a high presence. Course content is usually virtually the same in these as larger schools, and the smaller institutions tend to work more closely with organizations, affording you more opportunities to get in front of your target market. You want the recruitment exposure, and so do they.

As I mentioned earlier, I was once leading a recruitment campaign aimed at pharmacists, a very hard-to-fill position. There are eight schools in all of Canada that graduate pharmacists. The one in closest proximity to my organization was University of Toronto. We designed and launched our campaign there based upon getting physically *in front of* the students. U of T has an excellent website posting and career site, but our group decided that we wanted to get "face time" with the students, as many of them wouldn't yet know the benefits of working for our hospital.

The information session was a horrendous bust. Students just weren't interested. Even food didn't pull them in. When we researched why, the situation seemed dire: large private firms from across North America had targeted the Toronto campus and were offering huge hiring bonuses.

It turns out that, straight out of school, most graduates choose to follow the route of private pharmacy practice, in part due to the fabulous packages and on-campus marketing campaigns organized by companies such as Walgreens and

Shoppers Drug Mart. As well, a large centre like Toronto has a number of teaching hospitals close by (which are part of their educational rotations) that attract those students choosing to start their careers in hospital practice.

The final nail in the information coffin for us was that the Toronto campus is very urban in its student make-up. There was much less chance that a University of Toronto student would choose to join our rural organization for the simple fact that they relish the downtown urban life. We simply hadn't matched our employee value proposition with our target school.

Not long afterward, we targeted two of the smaller Universities that provide the same education and we were much more successful. We not only had face time, but we had interest. These students were not being hit as often with other corporate messages, and the students were mostly people that chose the smaller university *BECAUSE* it had a more rural feel. The community and school matched what we wanted to find in our employees.

When you are researching possible target schools, talk to the career centre at the school. Check out their program-specific and career websites, annual reports in magazines (in Canada, the annual *Macleans* magazine College & University Rankings can give you a good feel), and look to see what other "best practice" competitors are doing.

A Recruitment Marketing Plan

I have already covered the importance of marketing, and taking measures to increase your brand presence on campus. Now is the time to translate an overall strategy into realistic steps and plans.

Developed by your committee, a marketing plan can easily mesh with your overall recruitment campaign plan. This is when you examine *how* you deliver your message, and really detail the specific direction you intend to implement. Below is a checklist detailing a number of tactics that you can utilize; your committee will come up with others that are unique and important for your organization.

Set the marketing objectives of your campaign.

Examine your overall objectives – the ones you set with your recruitment group – and think about how they can be translated into marketing goals.

Identify whom you are targeting.

Using your Brand Features & Benefits chart, employee profiles, and target school determinations, fully document your target market. Back up your information with statistics wherever possible.

Determine how you will get your message out.

I have outlined a number of tactics for campaign success that will help with this step. You should also feel free to look at what is working for other organizations, what recommendations the university or college can provide, and what innovative activities are happening in the general recruitment environment.

Commit to timelines and frequencies.

Begin to match timelines with your plans. As with any good business plan or project plan, milestones must have timelines attached to them. The good thing about a campus campaign is that in many cases, imposed timelines may dictate your planning timelines or frequency of contacts. Be sure to not only research job fairs and interview times, but also graduations, registration testing, ad placements, and so on.

As you will read in the next section, the university's career centre is your friend. Use it especially to help guide your timelines. You don't want to be caught at an event while your target market is on a work experience placement.

Set a budget.

Be sure that direct and indirect costs for marketing specific-initiatives are rolled into the overall campaign budget.

Then Just Do it!

Chapter Four

TACTICS FOR
CAMPAIGN SUCCESS

Advertising

Advertising is the easiest and most often used technique in recruitment. Connected with other recruitment activities, it can be a very powerful means of delivering your message by actually soliciting applicants and building a brand base amongst target markets.

Brochures, information pamphlets and other marketing collateral

An easy way to promote your brand message on campus is to design and distribute promotional materials that link to your brand message. The message should identify who you are, why that is important to the audience, and how the audience can take advantage of your offering. Many companies stop their recruitment efforts at simply promoting the vacancies they have at that specific point in time on a posting board. Those postings are destined to be lost in a maze of other opportunities, or worse yet, never reach the target market in the first place. Savvy organizations know that they need to be front-of-mind throughout the year in order to keep the candidate pool interested There are many opportunities to promote your organization through inserts in college calendars, career center resource centres and web links through pop-up and other standard print "blotters."

Although the appeal of this type of method can be limited, it is essential that it be used in the early communication stages of a company's brand. This method of communication will link the organization to the message, and this can form the basis for ongoing development of that message.

At one organization I worked with, we wished to promote the lifestyle options and community involvement of our staff through campus advertising. We featured our employees during their "off work time," and their lifestyle choices were made the focus of our posters. Through these posters we aimed at driving traffic to our website, and from there were able to build a link to our message. The natural next step was to lead them to our career opportunities, all of this prior to a more significant on-site presence.

In designing the brochure consider these issues:

1. Design your brochure with your target market in mind, and match this with your overall recruitment plan. Are the target candidates all in one academic program? Is the market defined by a certain group of individuals? Or are your vacancies more broad in spectrum entry-level in nature?

2. Convey your features and benefits clearly in your brochure.

3. Think about other brochures you have seen and admired. What did you like about them? What design features could transfer to your brochure?

4. Think about the look and feel you want from your brochure. Think about what you are trying to communicate and how you will convey this alongside your main message.

5. Outsource the design and printing of your brochure if you do not have the in-house expertise and capabilities. Design is extremely important. A graphic designer can take your idea and make it into a professional, effective tool. If outsourcing is not an option, consult with your marketing department, if you have one, for ideas and suggestions.

6. Print glossy copies of the brochure and follow your marketing plan by using this versatile tool effectively.

The Job Fair

The job fair is the most obvious and most promoted career event on college campuses. Depending on the size of school, how general the job fair is and the experience level of the organizers, these events can vary from a small, intimate affair, to a large exhibition targeting thousands of individuals.

Using your marketing questions (Remember Chapter 3 – What is my target audience? Does it match this event?), it is important to gauge the expected effectiveness of an event for your organization. Remember, a job fair is a tool in your recruitment kit – not the only answer, but combined with other targeted efforts it could be a perfect opportunity to showcase your brand and build or enhance personal relationships with candidates.

Now think about this: What could be more powerful than a student getting personalized contact prior to the job fair, and then renewing that connection at a large event? In that case, as the organization, not only would you strengthen your position as a career choice, but you also will have showcased the connection in front of other candidates in a forum with your competitors.

There are some basics to cover before a job fair event actually takes place. (If you haven't been involved before, attend one to see how it works.) Start with your background – know it, remember it, apply it. Know your brand, and make sure that any representatives know your message.

And please, be sure that your reps are positive people that can make quick connections with others. Alumni are best, but not at the risk of compromising a positive impression. Be very aware of this!

Pre-fair Posters – Announce Your Arrival!

Remember when we talked about branding and the importance of building your brand recognition on campus? Pre-event ads are a perfect example of an underutilized, yet very effective tool to ensure continuous branding, and help draw event-day traffic to your booth.

In your posters, don't just say "Come see us at booth 34." Instead, deliver your message... drive your value proposition home!

The best time to put up your free pre-event advertising is just before a job fair or career event occurs. The "powers that be" generally allow more advertising in the lead-up to an event than they would otherwise. Be sure to incorporate an area in the poster for promotion of your event as well as how to get more information about the school itself. This offers a link between the school, your organization and the event, gets important contact information across, and also delivers on your brand image. At Peterborough Regional Health Centre, we took advantage of this opportunity by delivering posters of our own employees enjoying the area's lifestyle opportunities – a key part of our brand message.

Hand-out Flyers

Career boards and campus bulletin boards are often "jam-packed" with information. If it looks like your posters may get lost and miss the target market, you need to design effective flyers. Using similar concepts to a poster, put together a flyer that will attract curious students to your booth and website. You may want to find a "hook" or point of interest like a giveaway submission, a promise of key career information or a special informational guest. Distribute them in high traffic areas that your target students are most likely to frequent such as a program lounge, cafeteria, coffee kiosk or library. You can also approach professors for possible distribution ideas in a target class.

Booth

If attending a job fair, you must have a competitive booth. This doesn't mean it has to be huge and expensive but in must be in the same ballpark as your competition. There is nothing worse than a tabletop display that resembles a grade 6 science fair project next to a large display that takes up two fair space allocations.

I am not suggesting that you race into competition with the "big spenders," but do as much as you can with what you have. My move into the public sector demanded that I learn to craft greater work with fewer resources. Moving from recruitment budgets of hundreds of thousands of dollars, to one of just a fraction of that forced me to be innovative. Believe me – it can be done, and that innovation is essential if you are to build an effective presence on campus to compete with the big guys.

There are many companies that sell booths, pop-up displays and pull-up stands. Some do the graphics and others sell the backings only and not the creative touch. Again, this will usually be a budgetary decision, but my advice to you would be to maximize what you can with what you have.

Most booths are 10 feet or 8 feet. Since most spaces are 10X10, the 8 ft booth actually fits best within that space, allowing for some room for set-up. If this isn't practical, or you have a smaller budget that does not allow for a booth, the other option is a roll-up stand. In any version, design is very important. The look of your backdrop is what often pulls in a prospective candidate at a fair.

Always keep in mind ease of set-up and takedown. It will only take an event or two of "tearing down" an onerous display for you to regret not buying the easily collapsible variety. To get an idea of how this works, hang out 10 minutes after a fair or event, and witness the event-wide "take-down" competition that takes place.

Figure shows a sample display. This display is of the larger variety and is a standard job fair booth size. This one in particular collapses and is stored in the podium for storage. I am not one to use a podium anyway, but it can be handy to have if you don't have a table to display items.   Lots of companies provide this type of unit and this is probably a good representation of what you need in order to compete at an on-campus career fair. Discuss your needs with your sales representative and I am sure that they can help you fit a booth and design into your budget.

Think strategically about your set up.

Many presenters at job fairs will set a table up in front of the space as if they were displaying wares at a flea market. You are not doing this! You need to "pull in" traffic. Think strategically. Approach it like a marketer would.

James C. Allison

The first goal is to direct traffic into your booth space. Reposition the table, if you have one or need one for material, so that it frames the side of your booth space. Do this by gauging the direction from which people will most often approach the booth. This positioning not only makes material accessible for the recruiter to hand out during conversations, but it also funnels traffic into the booth and sets up a friendly inviting atmosphere at the booth.

Please – do not sit behind a table.

Nothing drives me crazy more than seeing a booth where two recruiters sit timidly behind a desk and consider that as active recruitment. If you look like ticket-takers at a 50/50 draw, don't expect to generate candidate traffic. Not only will you not generate an inviting atmosphere in that way, but job searchers looking for a vital and vibrant organization are not going to bother taking the time to visit your booth. Perception is reality to candidates at a job fair, and your first impressions are crucially important. Implore people to visit!

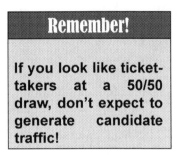

Remember!

If you look like ticket-takers at a 50/50 draw, don't expect to generate candidate traffic!

Your Reps!

As a recruiter in today's hiring environment the best tool you possess is your ability to make a connection with the student. This is the ultimate equalizer, and is what can turn into the nugget of advantage that puts your over the top.

Face-to-face communication is the best way to connect the dots for the candidate, to draw the line between what they want and what your organization can provide. If you have been trained in sales you will know the importance of linking a product's features and benefits with the needs and wants of the customer. The same is true for candidates and even more so for a campus candidate with minimal work experience.

The successful recruiter is one that can tailor and adapt the value statement to the candidate while still delivering upon the core branding. The recruiter must be able to develop personal relationships with all of the process players: the recruitment committee, the career centre staff, the candidates and the faculty.

> ## Remember!
>
> **Your reps must be positive, embody your brand, and link well with students. Alumni are good, but that alone will not define the link. The engaged employee with a passion for the organization, its workplace, its brand, and the job are the best selling tools you have. The ability to link with the students and the faculty is imperative.**

Ongoing Contact

The secret to success at any college job fair is what follows. Like so many experiences in business, the event can be staged very well, connections can be made, but the truly successful recruitment team knows that follow-through after the event is the key to winning the "Jackpot."

In today's environment, and the foreseeable future, high demand for skilled talent means that fewer and fewer students will come to events bearing resumes. They are at the event to collect information, to plan and make contacts. The candidates you really want **will** have options. You **must** make the connection and then continue contact.

How? Below are a number of constant-contact strategies.

Giveaways & Ballots

Lets remember that students at the events are still students. Money is scarce and they are big on food and free stuff. Offer an attractive giveaway, and you will have a busy booth all day long. The key is to collect contacts throughout the day to build a contact database. Use a ballot to collect contact info – and don't stop at the name and address. Get e-mail, area of study, hobbies, anything that you can use to personalize your ongoing communication. The more you can gather the better you can target. Below is a sample ballot to help you collect all the info you might want to capture.

Your Company Name
Name
Telephone
Email
Program & Year
Hobbies & Interests
Your Company Website & Logo

You might wonder why the hobby section is of interest. Think of it this way – what better way to make a personal link with candidates, and help them see why they should build a career with your organization, than by appealing to their personal interests? Let them know the interest options that are available through your place of work.

For instance, I live in a picturesque, lifestyle-oriented city. When I make contact with students that like mountain biking, I don't just give them info on the company, I add trail maps and invite the most promising to my city to experience the area, and see these activities that I intentionally link with the organization.

Giveaways should match your brand message. Since we promoted lifestyle at one organization I was with, we used things like carabineers with our website logo on them, waterproof personal item holders, pedometers and other lifestyle related items as "quick-hit" giveaways.

Career Centres

The Career Centre is an on-campus, educational instrument for students, and the good ones are often hubs for student job search activity for a wide variety of students. Centres often provide a number of services ranging from career counseling and workshops, to job postings and resume critiques. Most are very open to a strong relationship with key employers, not only for job fairs and formal events, but also for things like Career Development sessions, mentoring and practice interviewing.

The college career centre is key to your sustained on-campus program. Some feel that this group is an unnecessary middle stage between the candidate and the potential employer. I prefer to think of the career centre as a contact point that is also a wealth of information, and the more informed exposure, the better.

Treat the career centre as a client. Many groups make the mistake of only calling the career center representative once a year at job fair time. For the minimal work it takes, you should develop a relationship with your career center representative. These reps can help you identify opportunities to strategize your presence, and are a key link to the students you want to meet. They can keep you up-to-date on trends and provide competitive data that you would not normally get access to.

Be sure to check with the career centres at your target schools for innovative or unique opportunities to make contact with students. Take advantage of the opportunity to provide your expertise to students who you identify as candidates for your organization. Not only does this promote a "real-world" education relationship for students, but it helps your relationship with the career centre office, which is possibly your strongest point of contact on campus.

Remember!

Another reason to link with the career centre is TIMELINES.

Many organizations make the mistake of recruiting only in the final few months of the school year. In areas of high demand (for instance, marketing and pharmacy students) students may have accepted an offer prior to that timeframe. The career centre deals with all of the organizations that engage in on-campus recruiting efforts, and have a good idea of when students are having interviews (usually in the fall and winter), and when they make their final decisions. Don't waste your time. And certainly don't assume that your program was bad when your timing was simply off.

The career centre can also be a good source of comparison data. These centres can help you find the best time for an information session – sometimes it isn't the best plan to go toe-to-toe with the big guy! You can learn about the tactics employed by other organizations, and get suggestions regarding methods of recruitment that have worked in the past. Experts from career centres can also provide a list of definite things to do or include in your efforts, and what might be opportunities that have yet to be explored. Career service staff are knowledgeable and can help you get tied in to the school, key students and faculty. A positive relationship with this group is very important.

Some possible ways to partner with College Career Centres include:

- Job Fairs

- Career Counselors and Counseling Services

- Practice Interviews

- Networking Events or Alumni groups

- Job postings

- Candidate resume collection

- Information table booking and set-up

- Targeted internal communication to students

- Workshops

- Interview Scheduling

- Coordination of on-site events like Information sessions and Receptions

- Resume Development and Critiques

- ⮂ Mentoring programs

- ⮂ Placements and Job Shadowing

- ⮂ Company Information – *ensure that this is appropriate for your organization and that it extends your brand message.*

- ⮂ Consultation (such as advertising on-campus)

These are few ways to link-up with the important resources your Career Centre partner can provide, but don't stop there. Brainstorm together and you can create a mutually beneficial and productive relationship

On-campus Interviews

Pre-announcing your vacancies through advertised interviewing can be quite effective if you already have a recognizable name and positive reputation on campus. Be sure that you have a realistic idea of this before relying very heavily on this technique.

Many of the big industry players and consulting groups book interview times ahead of a scheduled event, and pre-interview key applicants to posted positions. Students love the practice and opportunity to showcase themselves for the big names, but don't put your organization in a compromising position by setting it up for a poor performance when up against the top competition. Before on-campus interviews can be successful, there must be a buzz, and energy and excitement built around your brand. This will allow you to compete and create the perception of an employer of choice.

If you are conducing on-campus interviews, they must be taken as seriously as on-site interviews. Make sure they are a stage-one interview (not 4 hours of testing and intense interviews) in front of a small team of trained representatives.

Remember: candidates will be comparing you with the interviewers from other firms. The more polished your group appears, the better your word-of-mouth publicity afterward.

Bring a lot of information about the job (job descriptions, peer testimonials or a representative that currently does the job) to an on-campus interview, and lots of information about your organization and community. If the candidate's resume has information that identifies pastimes, then bring information as personally targeted as possible. For example an MBA student I was interviewing loved sailing, so in that package I added information about the local yacht club and boating activities. My thought process was this – even if we didn't hire the individual, we increased the probability of her speaking positively about our workplace and interview.

Preparing for the interview:

1.   Fully prepare your interviewers

Ensure your interviewers are trained in behaviour-based interviewing. You will need a template of questions, but they need to understand probing techniques, and the link between past behaviour and predicting future performance. At the campus level you will make contact with a number of individuals that fit the technical or educational requirements of your job, but your interviewers need to find fit.

2.   Be sure your interviewers have your key messages and know your "elevator speech."

Your interviewers must have an understanding of the values, culture and vision of your organization. An immediate turnoff for students can be an inconsistent message and uninformed representatives. Your interviewers need to know answers, or be prepped on appropriate ways to deal with a question they don't know the answer to. Some organizations prepare for these questions by providing your recruiters with a list of Frequently Asked Questions to study. Failing that, have a method for "stumped" representatives to simply take the candidate's contact information and have an answer provided by the more appropriate person in the organization within a short period of time.

Remember: the interview is very much two-way "feeling out process" at this point.

3. Don't be pretentious – Period!

Behaviour-Based Interviews at a Glance:

Behaviour-based interviews are the most accepted and, in my opinion, effective means to gauge the future performance of an individual. It is well-worth providing full training on this subject to your recruitment team, but here is a quick overview of the concept and process.

Even during a campus process, interviews are an exercise that can be extremely uncomfortable for both the interviewee and the interviewer. A student may be intimidated by a full interview process because of inexperience with the process, anxiety surrounding implications on future career paths and options, and sometimes from a general lack of preparation for something that can be much more formal than expected.

For the interviewer, this can be like conducting a performance appraisal – an essential tool, but uncomfortable. The interviewer may never have received training or effective support through the process. Human Resources may have built a system for interviewing that was so onerous, structured and taxing that interviewees lose all desire to be engaged in the process. A good recruiter will spend time helping both parties prepare for the event by coaching Managers and letting candidates know what to expect. The more relaxed both parties can be, the more accurate the results of the interview.

Your managers may remember interviews that were based on a "gut feeling" and intuition. Maybe they used a checklist to check the "hard skills" of the candidate, and talked to the person for a while to gauge work ethic and personality. I would never say to rid an interview process of that "gut feeling" test, but both empirical studies and best practice results prove that a more structured, behaviour-based approach should compliment your instinct.

Behaviour-based interviewing has its roots in psychology and works under the basic premise that "past performance is the best predictor of future performance". If you have been to an interview in the last few years, or conducted many, chances are you have been exposed to this type of process. The interview questions now revolve around recalling specific examples of past behaviour and often begin with "tell me about a time when…". Candidates that have prepared for only the more traditional "tell me about your strengths" questions may be surprised with how pointed these questions are. These tough questions are meant to objectively determine real performance and the applicant's behavioural match with the profile of success for the job.

Step 1

Determine the competencies/behaviours that are key to the position. If you have already done this as part of your recruitment campaign planning, you will be well ahead at the interview stage.

To focus your efforts use the Successful Candidate Profile in Appendix A

Step 2

Standardized interview guide

An interview guide should be developed that outlines the behaviours required and has questions aimed at drawing out specific and detailed accounts of past behaviour that exhibits the candidates match to the job. A popular method of structure for answers (what the interviewer is looking for and that interviewee should be providing) is the **STAR Method**. For each question the candidate is asked to describe a:

S or T – Situation or Task

A – Action. What the candidate did

R – Result. The outcome of the actions and event.

If the interview is designed for the behaviours that have been outlined, the result should be a much more objective interview process that is truly based upon the job. From an organizational standpoint the results are targeted, valid, consistent, standardized and legal. All are important factors when interviewing.

As organizations begin to look towards using less tangible skills to determine longer term potential, the behaviour-based interview can be an excellent tool when evaluating fit for relatively inexperienced candidates. An open mind will lead to success, and a "tunnel vision" employer that only looks at the "hard skill" checklist will lose out in the interview process and in long run success.

One challenge you may find when interviewing a student candidate is that they may have little direct work experience. Behaviour-based interviewing helps with that challenge by taking into account similar past situations. College grads are often short on industry experience, but have great applicable experiences through summer jobs, volunteer positions and school projects. Be sure to open the examples up to these areas of experience and probe to find the behaviour examples you are looking for.

Information Sessions

Information sessions are standard practice for some disciplines and some programs. For others, information sessions can be a new and innovative method of branching out. Contact the career centre of the school you are interested in to get hints on holding sessions. Your intention would be to gain a captive audience with the purpose of providing details of career opportunities at your organization.

When I worked in the packaged goods industry, it was imperative to provide information sessions because the fierce competition for talent had made it standard practice for years.

Build it, and they shall come. When offering information sessions, remember to think of ways to entice students to your session. Food always brings students. You will boost your chances of a successful turnout by footing the bill for some food. Remember, for your first session or two at a site, you are building the excitement about your brand. Food and giveaways will help build that excitement.

In reflecting on my own experiences again, the lifestyle branding was the inspiration for a giveaway at an info session – a mountain bike. When they saw this, students came in droves. They didn't just look, they actively engaged with our representatives. And, we ended up hiring the attendee that won the bike. It really was a win-win!

Your reps are very, very important. As far as representatives are concerned, alumni and "like" individuals are very powerful at an event like this. If you can, bring positive employees that are alumni and promote and demonstrate a successful career for a recent graduate. You want the students to see themselves in a similar role and being able to connect the dots of the next steps in their career with a path in your organization. This can be very powerful. Also, your representatives should be trained to be ongoing contacts – their job shouldn't be done at the end of the session. They are, in fact, your best recruiters.

Give a presentation, not a lecture. At the information session, do give a presentation, but keep it short and entertaining. Students are in lectures all day... they don't want to hear one from someone who isn't responsible for their grades. Educate them about your organization, your brand, your value proposition, and sample employee paths through real-life examples if possible. Tell them why they might fit with your organization. Find a hook. If you can talk about an issue that is important or familiar to the group, you can attract a larger crowd and provide an experience that students will appreciate.

Always be sure to have an entertaining, informed speaker. Yes, it is great to have the CEO deliver the message, but only if that person is a powerful speaker. If you have to go a level or two down from CEO to find an engaging speaker – do it. The CEO can be there, but don't put the crowd to sleep in order to have the "top dog" deliver the presentation.

Interaction, interaction, interaction. The old real estate adage about location can be turned to something very useful when it comes to interaction and relationships. Make interaction opportunities a priority in an information session. Set up time both before and after a presentation for students to interact with your representatives.

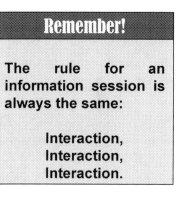

Remember!

The rule for an information session is always the same:

Interaction,
Interaction,
Interaction.

In campus recruiting, it always applies that personal interaction is paramount. People entering a career field love to speak with people who are experiencing the field first hand. Be sure to facilitate that experience for them.

The space must be enticing. Spend the time to ensure that the room you have for your information session feels right. The size and ambiance should facilitate personal interaction, food should be delivered on time, and details should be seamless.

Finally, find a way to get contact names and means of thanking them for their attendance. Again giveaways with ballots are a clever way to do this.

Internships & Co-op Placements

Internships, placement opportunities and co-ops are powerful ways to recruit and brand. "Real life exposure" is a part of many academic programs, prior to graduating.

In the past, placements were something the employer did as a gesture of good will, or as a way to get cheap labour for projects. Many organizations are now realizing that these placements are terrific *opportunities*. Some organizations have set-up a coordinating body for these internships. The approach is to treat them as much as a recruiting effort as a learning experience for the student. When they happen, the organization gets the opportunity to observe and evaluate the possible candidate in a specific work setting while being able to promote the organization;' brand message. In a best-case scenario, the student returns to campus with that message in hand, and also works out as a working candidate upon graduation.

Set up an educational or co-op program at your place of work. If you haven't already been doing placements then you should begin contacting your target markets and offer your organization as a placement opportunity. If you already are, take a good, hard and objective look at your program. Is it coordinated? Does it reinforce your Value Proposition? Does your plan involve continuous contact? Do players within the organization regard the placement as a recruitment tool? A "no" to any of these questions represents an opportunity!

The learning opportunity has to be a positive one. You don't want a student to have a terrible experience on placement and carry that message back to the campus. A negative experience can greatly injure your recruitment efforts. It may already be happening and you don't know it!

Get to know the people who are teaching students within your organization. Survey the students after their placements. Survey faculty and students on campus, and find out their impressions. By offering placements, you need to be sure that the education your workplace provides is excellent, and that the relationships built through it leave the student feeling optimistic about the organization. Doing this requires commitment and time, so be sure that both are there throughout the organization. Otherwise you may be doing more harm than good.

Consider training for preceptors/managers. Many employees haven't had training in basic adult education. Some within your organization may not even understand your recruitment message or current educational relationships. It is a good investment, if you wish to build your reputation, to educate your "teachers."

Two past colleagues of mine put together a great preceptor-training plan for nurses called a *Guided Learning Program*. Bev Hill and Susan Redhead have done a great job developing the program, which weaves together the important components of a student-preceptor relationship, while keeping it fun and entertaining for all. The program is one of the base documents now used to develop a program sponsored by the Registered Nurses Association. This program has turned out to be another great branding opportunity for our organization, and a great way to build the campus program.

Sponsorships

Sponsorships are a great way to increase your organization's presence on campus. Sponsorships offer the opportunity to build a co-beneficial relationship with the school, while subtly boosting your presence in a constructive manner.

Students are becoming very sophisticated job researchers and will see a difference between blatant advertising and a sponsorship. Remember that Generation Next is very charity-minded, and a company that sponsors and adds value to the school experience may have a branding advantage on campus.

There are lots of opportunities to link your name with campus events.

➲ Be a conference Gold Sponsor.

Many conferences and recruitment fairs have educational components. Your organization can be positioned as not just an advertiser, but a contributor, often at a cheaper rate. I think of a time when a small print insert in an attendee package was about twice the price of buying a mountain bike to provide as a sponsor raffle! For that price came the insert, presentation of the bike at a dinner event with all attendees, and promotion throughout the event. Now that was Value! Sometimes it pays to sponsor.

➲ Be a Project Sponsor.

Post-secondary education is often very focused on project-based work (especially MBA programs) with "real-world examples" and case studies. What a perfect way to link with a target program, build your brand and educate students about your industry and company workings!

Linking as a project sponsor can be as simple as providing information for a case-study specific to your organization, to as detailed as providing a prize to a winning group in a case competition. If you compare the cost of this against the expensive advertising fees in industry publications, you will find that a targeted case study that immerses possible candidates in your organization's culture and business can be invaluable exposure for a very small investment.

Develop a case study scenario where the final work will benefit your organization. Involve members of your recruitment team and top management as part of the judging team, and have a presentation ceremony of the final award in front of the entire target group. You can't get that kind of exposure in your market in many other ways, and for such a moderate cost. Putting all this together takes a commitment on behalf of the organization, but this could possibly be one of the most potent, and overlooked tools available to you, regardless of the size of your firm.

➲ Be a guest speaker or panelist.

The depth of involvement as a guest speaker or panelist can vary. A small, local college may relish the opportunity to have a local employer visit a lecturer and tell students about what to expect in the workplace, and about the characteristics that employers look for in potential candidates. If the school's program head has not thought about the benefits of this type of session – educate him or her. Not only does the opportunity allow you to give back to the students and help them prepare for tough decisions ahead, but it also allows you a captive audience to introduce them to you and what YOU specifically look for in successful applicants.

Remember, recruitment is a two-way decision. You want students to fit your model, but they need to see that the model fits for them. It takes both for a new employee/employer relationship to work.

➲ Be a Mentor:

Being a mentor can be formalized or quite informal. Many universities have formalized programs of mentorship.

For instance, University of Toronto has a mentoring program and an Extern program. The first is an ongoing professional relationship that facilitates continual contact, coaching and advice to a specific student. The second, the Extern program, is a 5-day "on-site" shadowing experience. Neither requires financial commitment from the employer – just time. These kinds of mentorship interactions can be a great experience for both the student and the mentor.

Consider using a high-potential employee in the role of mentor for a student. The opportunity will provide a career development occasion for the employee, while exercising a recruitment and branding tactic directed at a target student.

➲ Help Organize a Welcome Event:

Organizing a get-together for target students, or sponsoring a "hospitality suite" before a job fair is an excellent way to promote your organization and brand. This subtle recruitment technique sets you up for major name recognition at a subsequent event. Add impact by providing a giveaway, or samples, to the attendees. Above all, make the event *fun* so that it is not received as a "hard-sell recruitment" event.

Workshops

Colleges and university career centers and liaison offices are often very receptive to individuals or organizations that want to help students learn about career development, job-searches or skills development. A workshop delivery not only helps students, but also offers a unique opportunity to link with them in their job preparation. Resume workshops and critiques, job search overviews, or networking educational sessions are examples of common workshops that organizations or individuals get involved in. A sample agenda for a workshop follows:

Sample Agenda

8:30 am (30 min)

Introduction

Overview of the current job market:

- make it interactive, ask questions, compare experiences

- be sure to mention your organization, but don't overpower

9:00am (30 min)

Review resume formats

Review template tools and effectiveness

- *many students now use Word and other templates to create their resumes. Show them how to choose an effective one, and put the content together. If you don't know how to build a resume yourself or just feel uneasy about teaching others how to do it, research career sites like Monster.com, Careerbuilder.com and Workopolis.ca. They all have excellent resources to get you comfortable with the formats and what works best.*

9:30 am (30 min)

Work through techniques (such as using action terms and highlighting specific outcomes)

Break

9:45 – close

Present samples and have attendees prepare or begin to amend their resumes

Added services such as resume critiquing can be very helpful for ongoing contacts and to increase positive exposure on campus.

Send E-cards and Thank Yous

Using the information you gather on your ballots at sessions, and resumes that you collect through all of your on-campus strategies, send thank-you e-cards to people who visit your booth and event. The more personal you make the notes the better, but any contact is positive.

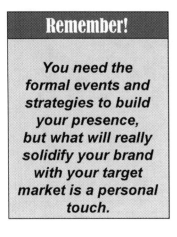

Remember!

You need the formal events and strategies to build your presence, but what will really solidify your brand with your target market is a personal touch.

If yours is a small firm that cannot produce a professional looking e-card, check out a website like bluemountain.com to see if they have an appropriate template. Failing that, send an e-mail and personalize it as much as possible.

Direct Mailings

Yes, the big D word.

Direct mail is not always a bad thing. In the case of student recruiting, it can be very effective. For specific target markets within your plan, and for very specific vacancies, this method can be valuable. Rather than "carpet bombing" your message, you can use direct mail to target specific lists. To start, you'll need a method of distribution, a message devise (such as a brochure or email), and access to the target market.

On campus, you get this access in a number of ways. The career centre can get you lists if they are able to under school policy. Often the program head or student program president is the best source of help for this. Student blogs, newsletters or plain ole' e-mail lists can be accessed through a relationship with these people. Call them. Even if they don't get you the list, they will often carry the message to the group.

If you find difficultly accessing a contact list, check the internet. An advanced search can often garner a great list of students, free of charge. A seasoned recruiter can help you with this. Many are very willing to teach you the tricks of the trade. I have a recruiter on my team that is a master at this – and he is continually surprised with the access to lists that he gains through the web. If you personally don't have this skill-set or you can't source it in your organization, find a headhunter and ask them to teach you. Many are very willing to teach you these little tricks of the trade.

Finally, you can often purchase lists through professional organizations that your target population may belong to, or general lists that are available trough publication houses or research organizations.

However you access the students, be sure that your message is beneficial to them, and that it is concise, respectful and gets the message across.

Internet and Your Career Website

You must think of your organization's website as the single most important recruiting tool in your on-campus kit.

The World Wide Web is where the playing field is much more level in the recruitment game. Sure, the big guys like Proctor & Gamble have a huge, flashy college recruiting site, but even the smaller player can make an impact with a well-designed site.

The reality is that today's students do the majority of their career research online. How your organization represents itself on the web can make or break your campaign. Truly. The web is THE primary way you can market your brand, your career opportunities and convey your Value Proposition to students.

Keys to a good website:

➲ **Have a separate Careers area that is easy to get to from the home page.**

One click should take you there. The highest traffic area on most websites is now the career section, so make it easy to find!

➲ **Link career information with your brand and career development paths.**

➲ **Give them "quick hit info."**

A mistake that many organizations make is taking wordy documents and data and merely uploading them. Think about writing for the internet – succinct, targeted and easy to navigate. If you need help, get it (the website www.askoxford.com has a great internet "better writing" overview). Include information that is important to your target audience, and it needs to be easily accessible, a quick read and in a web-friendly format. If you don't have experience with this, look at the websites of larger companies with developed career sites like Baptiste Health (http://www.ebaptisthealthcare.org/Careers) or Edward Jones (http://www.edwardjonesopportunity.com)

‣ **Personalize it.**

By reading your organization's website, candidates should feel like a part of the team. Remember to design it for ease of use. Make writing short, to the point and in colloquial language.

‣ **Advertise your web address everywhere!**

Drive your site. It is better to have people come to you, rather than your having to pull them there. In fact, this can be an evolution and measure of success for an effective site.

‣ **Offer an online application option.**

In-class Sessions and Expert Lectures

Many colleges and universities crave in-class guest lecturers from the field. Explore opportunities to guest lecture at target organizations. If you are able to deliver a sound and interesting presentation on a topic of expertise, this not only allows you to have a face-time link with students, but you also boost your brand by positioning your organization as an expert in the field. Everyone wants to work with an expert organization that has a good reputation. When are you identified as an expert in a classroom forum, people will make the association between expert and your organization.

On-site Recruitment Open House

Holding an open house is another trend that is used by large organizations in recruitment efforts. The open house allows the organization to build its brand through positive and controlled public relations. These forums are advertised through invitations pasted in classic advertising venues, and are really run like a mini, customized job fair. If this method is right for your organization (consider the size of your organization – are you too small?, the location appeal and the people and monetary resources required to pull off an excellent event) , a full process outlining how to hold an open house is listed below. As you can probably tell from my cautionary statements, I believe that an open house can be powerful, but only for some organizations. If your location is less than appealing or you are small enough that a targeted recruitment campaign makes more sense, stay away from this format. However, if it fits then go for it! Here's how:

Getting Ready

1. Organize a planning group using members of the recruitment committee for consistency.

2. Match the plans, goals and message for the open house with your organization's overall marketing plan.

3. Create an agenda for the open house that highlights your organizational features and benefits. Be sure to set an agenda that will allow for maximum attendance – not during key class time!

4. Create an event-specific budget

5. Have keynote speakers, interactive workshops and informal conversations that highlight your organization and work partners. Give students a valuable experience.

Location

1. Ensure that you have appropriate transportation available, as required. For instance, do you need to reserve buses or set up additional parking facilities?

2. Contact campus connections and ensure that your chosen timing, agenda and location are as convenient as possible.

Staffing the Event

1. Have enough event staff available. Use committee members, school alumni and volunteers.

2. Train and prepare staff with logistics and employee propositions. You can use a similar training plan to the one you developed for your recruitment committee.

3. Use your agenda and plan to assign specific duties to your open house staff.

Logistics

1. Set up a welcome table with a sign-in sheet to collect contact information for post-open house communication and thank you.

2. Create and hand out information packages with day-specific details and recruitment brochures, website information, and other pertinent information.

3. Be sure to have many "first-contact individuals" to welcome guests and direct traffic. *Remember: this is a recruitment event and you need to make the one-on-one connections.* Enlist current employees to help with the open house, people who can answer questions and make connections.

4. Provide food and refreshments, and have staff in the food area to converse with attendees in an informal setting.

5. Have attendees fill out an evaluation to help evaluate the effectiveness of the event, but also provide an opportunity to instigate contact after the event with a thanks you for providing feedback.

Celebrate!

1. Publicly thank the team, and celebrate success!

2. Thank attendees for coming to the open house.

3. Thank partners and school staff for their assistance in making the event a success.

The Best and The Rest

The techniques outlined above are all aimed at creating the most positive and successful campus campaign for you as possible, regardless of the size of your organization. When Career Centre staff members across Canada were asked what separated the best companies from the rest on campus the following traits were identified.

8 Traits of Top Campus Recruiting Organizations – According to Career Centres

1. Organized
2. Involved
3. Open-Minded
4. Consistent Presence
5. Knowledgeable
6. Offer Good opportunities
7. Include Career Centres
8. Ethical and Honest

The Biggest Mistakes

1. Unfriendly/Rude/Intimidating
2. Misrepresentation/Over-promise
3. Uninterested/Bored
4. Not following up with students as promised
5. Fail to advertise enough (or early enough)
6. Change recruiting staff frequently
7. "Disappear" during low recruitment times
8. Unprepared/Ill-informed

Source: *Learning to Work Study 2004*
D-Code /Brainstorm

Consistency and Visibility –
Common Themes for Success.

If you employ a number of the techniques outlined in the Chapter, you will greatly improve your chances at being on of the top recruiting organizations on campus.

Chapter Five

CLOSING THE DEAL

The On-site Visit...Closing the Deal!

The on-site visit refers to the moment with the potential candidate visits your workplace. The main goal of this visit is to determine the fit between the candidate and the team. It is also a final opportunity to woo the person that may be ready to entertain offers from a number of competing organizations.

Where many organizations lose out at this stage is by not recognizing that they are still being interviewed at the on-site visit. Candidates in hard-to-fill fields and professions are now moving to a mindset that asks the question "Why do I want to work for you?" You and your team must be able to answer that question positively while simultaneously assessing that person's fit in your team. These combined tasks make the on-site visit very important.

The Tour

Start with a tour of the facility. Don't forget – make it fun and interesting!

Showcase your highlights, and be sure to focus on those areas that are important to the candidate. The aim is to give the candidate a dose of reality, and show the true colours of the job and work environment. That said, be sure to control the experience. Like any marketing initiative, the success of the on-site visit will be measured by connecting the real experience with the highlighted marketing message. Show how your brand becomes reality at your organization, but be sure that the message is delivered professionally.

If possible, link the candidate with "buddies" for the day. Use employees that are positive, and excellent examples of your work culture, and prepare those employees ahead of time to understand your marketing message.

The Interview

Decide upon the interview process that you will conduct during the on-site visit, but reflect in that process your positioning in the marketplace. Is it most appropriate to have multiple formal interviews, a mix of shorter interviews or a casual meet and greet with the direct team or work group? This decision really depends upon your organizations hiring process, work culture and the level of interest of your candidates.

Bigger, more established companies often use an on-site visit for complex interviews, such as case studies, or having the candidates present in a high stress, realistic job environment. Think about whether you are positioned to do this, from a brand perspective and from the perspective of your position in the marketplace.

In any event, be sure to make the candidate feel like they will fit into the organization's culture, if in fact you have decided that they will. Offer social interactions. Get them interested and even invested in the work the organization does, and the city and community. Set up a social interaction event for the candidate such as a sporting event, dinner theatre, or something even more customized to your community.

The Offer

Be Prepared. Especially in hot job market programs, you must be prepared to present an offer and strike while the iron is hot. That offer could come when they are on site for a final interview, or directly after that visit.

In highly sought after programs, it is not abnormal for the student to receive a number of offers at once. Don't miss that timeline! The candidate may hold onto your offer while looking at competitor deals, so the feelings linked with the offer are extremely important. Be sure to act quickly and connect your offer with a positive organizational culture experience.

Research your Offer. Be sure that you are "in the ballpark" when you offer a candidate a proposition. Final job search decisions are not traditionally made on compensation alone, so you must be competitive in other ways.

Generally speaking students have more sensitivity to direct finances, considering their financial burdens when leaving college or university. So while you most definitely can lose a candidate easily with an uncompetitive financial offer, a fit with the job, learning environment and work culture are also prevailing decision-makers.

Show everything that could be a decision factor. In your offer, include details that may be outside of your normal offer letters. Those things that may be standard practice at your facility like succession planning programs, learning opportunities or wellness programs should be included in your offer letter. A

Remember!

Recruitment is nothing without retention!

candidate that has not worked extensively in the field may need this information in order to make a fully informed decision. Showcase the special areas that demonstrate opportunities to learn, and that the organization is a challenging workplace. These details are paramount to today's youth.

On-Boarding

Recruitment without retention is pointless. An organization can no longer assume that employees will stay with them for their entire career, but keeping good employees in organization as long as possible should be a goal of every company. The cost of losing an employee is massive; cost of turnover estimates range from 50 to 150% of the person's salary, depending on the vacancy's difficulty to hire and the investment in the individual through training and so on. Regardless of which percentage is right, the investment you make in a new hire is substantial.

In my mind, creating a positive experience during the initial few weeks of hire is where the final closing of the recruitment phase actually occurs. Many people will say recruitment transfers the person to retention efforts upon the candidate's start date, but my feeling is that the recruitment team provides a real sense of familiarity for the candidate and, therefore, needs to play a role in the successful integration of the new hire into the company culture. Do you remember how you felt during your first few weeks in a new job? Do you remember how a familiar face made you feel during that time, when you may have been feeling a little lost? That little bit of familiarity and friendliness can make the difference between a successful new employee and early turnover. Another positive impact of this interaction is that the emotional investment in helping the employee succeed becomes even deeper.

Some keys to a successful on-boarding process:

1. Have a structured orientation process. Having an agenda of learning, a list of key contacts and scheduled social interactions with bosses and co-workers (mix in some members of the recruitment team) is extremely important. Even hires that love change crave order and structure while they observe and get acclimated to a new environment. If these people get a copy of an agenda before their first day you will look like an organized operation that values its new hires.

2. Be very prepared for their first day. This must be a priority! Lasting impressions are gathered on the first day and a welcoming environment goes a long way to engaging new employees. Standing in a hallway or being left at a desk for hours does a lot to disengage an employee early on in their tenure.

3. Have the new hire's office or workspace fully prepared. Have a full set of office supplies, a welcome note and contact lists available for them. Give them time to set it up as they find comfortable.

4. Assign a "Buddy" to your new hire. This person should be someone of the same or similar level of the new hire. That buddy should be a resource for the new hire as well as a support outside the "line supervisor," and be sure to use the same principles you used when determining recruitment committee members. Buddies are the face or your organization, so they must be committed to providing a positive experience to the new hire. Buddies should represent your culture and should check-in with the employee consistently for the first 4-6 weeks of their employment.

5. Evaluate! Ask your new hires what they think about your on-boarding process. They can give you valuable

information about improvements you can make to the process as well as positive feedback regarding what you are doing right.

Be sure the positive on-boarding of new hires is a priority for everyone on your team.

Chapter Six

EVALUATING THE EFFECTIVENESS OF YOUR CAMPAIGN

As with any business initiative, it is imperative to measure the impact of your program, and tie the results to your organizational goals. There are a number of ways to do this with a recruitment campaign, and you should pick and choose the measures that make sense for your organization, and best illustrate the desired effects of your program.

Metrics packages should not be a cookie-cutter plan, but rather a way to analyze results and enable your organization to back up its actions in a business case. I am big proponent of measurement, but not measurement overkill. Apply metrics to your goals, and measure what is important. Do not measure for the sake of measurement.

The following are some possible metrics that your organization can consider using to determine the effectiveness of its actions, and build a consistently better campaign.

Applicant Source

How many times have you placed ads in the paper, been approached by a recruitment agency offering to help you source candidates, or tried a really cool innovative approach to reaching your target market?

The answer to at least a couple of these questions is probably "lots of times!" Now if I asked you how successful each was, would you be able to definitively show me the answer. Better yet, have you shown your CEO those success rates? If you can't get past "I think so," then you have the opportunity to *really* show the impact that you can and will make on your business by running an effective and targeted campaign.

Start by tracking the areas in which your organization is finding success today. This is essential. Every campaign starts as an educated guess, and then focuses over time to become a talent magnet. You need to know where your efforts are being successful in order to build upon and identify your competitive advantages.

Remember: these identified areas will change over time. Be sure that you are always reviewing these results, and be prepared to rethink your prize ideas. They may look good on paper, but you need to have results.

Hire Source

In order to determine the success of marketing techniques and specific recruitment channels, it can be very helpful to track hire sources. The detail of these statistics depends on how granular you wish to go, but the bare minimum standard should indicate the number of the current years' hires that were sourced through job fairs, advertising, and direct mail. As you become more sophisticated with your data, you can track back to specific marketing campaigns and tools. Another great instrument in your business plan arsenal is the ability to show direct success from specific efforts.

Be sure to include a question for every candidate at hire that addresses how they found out about the job. Don't assume you know their answer. Many recruiters make the mistake of assuming that they originally made contact with the candidate.

You do your marketing plans an injustice by doing making this assumption. As you explore more indirect branding methods, you may find that more and more candidates may have indirect source answers.

Cost per Hire

Definition: Total Recruitment Cost/# of hires

A common way for organizations to gauge both campaign effectiveness and recruitment value is through cost per hire. This statistic must be used in conjunction with other stats to paint the whole picture (for example, harder-to-fill positions may justifiably experience higher costs).

The most common calculation for this measurement is to take your campus campaign costs and divide that by the number of hires. The result is a per-hire cost allocation that allows for comparison by position, recruitment stream and venue.

Acceptance Rate

Definition: Offers/Acceptances of Offers

This is a great statistic for gauging your offer competitiveness and ultimate success on specific campuses. When I worked in packaged goods, a key goal for us was to improve our acceptance rate.

There were two reasons that this was important to us: 1) it helped us understand the competitiveness of our offer and employee value proposition as compared to other tier-one competitors; and 2) it forced us to add to our hiring practice picture the issue of fit. An accepted offer points to a good fit not only from the organization's perspective, but also from the candidate's. If a candidate accepted our offer in the wake of a number of other offers, we knew that our value proposition and offer were, most likely, a good fit for that individual. This is, of course, only a piece of determining success, but it can be a key component of any analysis.

Brand Recognition

This statistic is much more difficult to evaluate and determine, and may be important to large companies or those in heavy competition with other firms in the target marketplace. What this stat aims to measure is the recognition of the organization amongst a group of possible candidates. Naturally, this stat will change over time, hopefully in a positive way. In order to truly see the value of this measure, the organization would need to collect repeated data over time over a number of complete recruitment cycles.

Companies collect brand recognition data in a number of ways. Good examples of this are:

a) Name and Message Recognition: Through surveys the target market should show an increased awareness of your organization and be able to link your brand or work benefits with the name.

b) Employee Referral Rate: Whether the organization has an informal referral program or not, if a high number of referred employees say that employees are recommending the workplace, then the brand is extending outside the facility's walls, and the organization is being viewed as an engaging employer.

c) Application Source: This is measured by the number of applications coming in from targeted programs and schools. Successful campaigns will find a direct difference associated with brand-building activities on campus.

d) Turnover Rate of High Potential Employees: Exit interviews may help determine if your organization needs to fine-tune its message to match reality. If the two are not aligned, an option is to work on making the brand a reality internally. The fact is that recruitment is futile without retention.

e) Web Hits and Unique Users: Successful brands will find an increase in web activity over time. This activity should also peak when specific campus initiatives are underway and are driving traffic to the site.

Student Hire Retention Rate

Definition: Percentage Student Hires retained by Pre-set Date.

This is the "did the rubber hit the road" statistic. Any of these metrics in isolation can lead the organization astray, but in combination they can be very powerful tools.

You can work to increase the hire numbers, your brand recognition and your value proposition, but none of that will be beneficial if you siphon your new hires through the workforce within the first year. Don't expect "lifers" out of the new crop of students, but do expect to keep your new hires long enough to show them off on campus the next year.

Age and Tenure at Departure

Are you doing a good job managing the different generations that you are bringing into the organization? This retention statistic is an important barometer when looking at how you are mixing the generations within your organization. No college recruitment campaign can be fully and adequately evaluated without considering the trend of departures.

Volume of Applications

Acknowledge the efforts of your team! Show them that their hard work is appreciated.

For an organization looking to increase both presence and its overall pool of applicants, this can be a metric of choice. In my opinion, it merely measures action and not results, but tied with other measures it serves a great purpose.

My preference, when an organization moves beyond quantity to a strategic recruitment effort, is to consider both the volume and the quality applications and actual hires.

Application Quality

This statistic can be difficult to evaluate. However, effort to standardize and track this statistic is an important move toward demonstrating the worth of a campaign, and the link recruitment has with actual results.

Though relatively unscientific, you should see an improvement in the basic qualifications of each application. You can quickly show the impact of targeted recruitment efforts by highlighting the higher percentage of qualified applicants. This is where quantity can quickly be outmatched by quality through niche candidate targeting. You move from what recruiters like to call "a carpet-bomber" to a "smart target" recruiter.

For additional ideas and comparative data, a number of industry specific agencies provide benchmarking data. Good sources of this type of information are the *Saratoga Institute* founded by measurement guru Jack Fitz-Enz, and *The Human Resources Benchmarking Guide,* a book authored by Colin Dawes, a Canadian Human Resources Benchmarking expert, published by Carlson.

Make The Case!

Start collecting historical data. Keep in mind that you will be selling these efforts to upper management, employees and other stakeholders. Comparative data will allow you to highlight "quick wins." Not only will you be able to track progress, but you will also begin to formulate changes and future successes almost immediately.

Chapter Seven

SAMPLES & RESOURCES

The following section is a collection of tools, templates and resources that will help you prepare and organize your campaign. We tried to add a few basic forms as well as an innovative idea or two. I am always open to hearing about, and sharing, more ideas and tools to help connect talent with talent-seekers. Feel free to share your expertise and idea with us at:

talentlinkpublishing@rogers.ca

Sample Career Centre Information Update Letter

Form 1

DATE:
KEY CONTACT
CAREER SERVICES
ADDRESS

Dear (Contact Name):

Thank you for including (Your Company) in your career planning and job search information and activities. Yourco understands the value of adding new graduates to our team, and that an ongoing relationship with your institution is mutually beneficial. We hope to develop that relationship even further.

Enclosed you will find several posters that highlight career opportunities at Yourco and our workplace culture. Your assistance in posting the information on bulletin boards accessible to students would be appreciated. We hope to generate interest in our organization, and provide a link to possible opportunities that match your student's career pursuits. Students will have the opportunity to visit our website to see career opportunities at our facilities, and learn more about exciting organizational developments.

Thank you for your consideration, and I look forward to speaking with you about opportunities to further develop the relationship between your students, the career center and Yourco.

Yours Truly

James Allison

Yourco

Student Feedback Form

Form 2

Your feedback is important to us. Please take a moment to fill out this short survey regarding the factors behind your career decisions. We hope to use this information to improve our hiring practices in the future in order to recruit even more top talent to our team!

Please rate by importance the following company qualities in regards to their influence on your decision to join a company after graduation.

1 = Not important
3 = Somewhat Important
5 = Very Important

Compensation

1   2   3   4   5

Reputation

1   2   3   4   5

Vacation

1   2   3   4   5

Good Mgt/Peer team

1   2   3   4   5

Treatment in recruitment process

1   2   3   4   5

Innovation

1   2   3   4   5

Work environment

1   2   3   4   5

Location/area

1   2   3   4   5

Unionized

1   2   3   4   5

Ongoing Education support

1   2   3   4   5

Work/life balance

1   2   3   4   5

Training and support

1   2   3   4   5

What turns you off a company
What do you see will be the biggest challenge in a new position
Which organizations do the best job recruiting on your campus
What makes them successful?
How do you research organizations?
What additional information would you like to receive about us that we didn't provide?
What would separate us from other companies in your job search?

Career Centre Feedback Form

Form 3

What could we have done to be a more effective presence?
What do you recommend we add to our recruitment package to better inform you or students about what we have to offer?
Can you suggest any other opportunities to link with students that we have yet to take advantage of?
How could we do that?
Are their any sponsorship or branding opportunities that you recommend we be involved in?
Any other general feedback or suggestions?

Successful Employee Profile

As outlined in the campaign preparation section of this book, it is essential to understand the job and what a successful employee "looks like" Use this tool to help discover and define that profile.

Form 4

Is there a job description?

-Review the description with the team, hiring manager and employee if possible

What are the competencies required for the position?

-Review skills, abilities, knowledge, experience

What would the ideal college entry level candidate be?

-Determine matching skills, abilities, knowledge, experience – keep in mind the experience level of new grad

What is the succession plan for the position?

-What is the career path and how will you fill the position if it is followed in the future?

What behaviours and traits will not work in this position?

-Use this to determine additional "fit" questions

Do we have "model employees to use as at recruiters for this role?

What does the ideal candidate want in a role?

-Recruitment is a two-way process – you need to meet the candidate's needs as well.

Recruitment Team Goal Checklist

Form 5

The Goals: What does success look like? Remember – use the SMART principles
Actions: The goals are broken down into very specific, time-bound actions to achieve the larger goal. Determine the specific tasks and sub-tasks required.
The Team: The group and the sponsor
Advertising, Branding and Sourcing Targets (link with marketing plan)
Budget
Supports required.
Communications plan

Chapter Eight

Suggested Reading & Resources

Books

1.   Secrets Of Power Marketing

Peter Urs Bender and George Torok | THE ACHIEVEMENT GROUP | May 1999

2.   Secrets of Power Presentations

Peter Urs Bender | THE ACHIEVEMENT GROUP | January 1999

3.   The Brand You50 (reinventing Work)

Tom Peters | Alfred A. Knopf | September 1999

4.   The Project50 (reinventing Work)

Tom Peters | Alfred A. Knopf | September 1999

5.   Re Imagine: Business Excellence in a Disruptive Age

Tom Peters | Dorling Kindersley | October 2003

6.   Winning The Talent Wars

Bruce Tulgan | W.W. Norton | January 2001

7.   High-Impact HR: Transforming Human Resources for Competitive Advantage

James C. Allison

David S. Weiss | John Wiley & Sons | February 1999

8.   *The First 90 Days: Critical Success Strategies for New Leaders at All Levels*

| Michael Watkins | Harvard Business School Press | September 2003

9.   *Purple Cow: Transform Your Business by Being Remarkable*

| Seth Godin | Portfolio Trade | May 2003

10.   Secrets of Face to Face Communication: How to Communicate with Power

| Peter Urs Bender and Robert Tracz | January 1999

11.   The Leader's Digest: Timeless Principles for Team and Organization Success

| Jim Clemmer | April 2003

12.   Guerrilla Marketing for Free: Dozens of No-Cost Tactics to Promote Your Business and Energize Your Profits

Jay Conrad Levinson | Houghton Mifflin Company | April 2003

13.   The Pig And The Python

| David Cork | Prima Publications | January 1998

Website Resources

http://www.vault.com

http://www.wetfeet.com

http://www.trentu.ca/admin/careers/students/links.html

http://www.cacee.com

http://www.Hrpao.org

http://www.shrm.com

http://www.talentlink.ca

http://www.monstertrak.monster.com/

http://www.cibcwm.com/wm/careers/campus-recruitment.html

http://www.caps.mcgill.ca/

http://www.trentu.ca/admin/careers/employers/

http://www.workopolis.com

http://www.jobpostings.ca

http://www.brainstorm.ca

http://walmartstores.com

http://www.edwardjonesopportunity.com/

http://www.cisco.com/web/about/ac40/about_cisco_careers_
home.html

http://www.ebaptisthealthcare.org/Careers/

If you know of any good resources or have used interesting campus
recruitment techniques, please send them along to TalentLink

e-mail talentlink@rogers.ca

About James (Jamie) Allison

Jamie Allison is an author and resource for Talentlink Business Publications, a strategic management resources firm that specializes in bringing together organizations, talented individuals and great ideas.

Mr. Allison's human resources career has included leadership and professional positions in retail, healthcare, technology, packaged goods and entertainment. He is a sought-after speaker with extensive recruitment, organizational effectiveness and employment branding experience. He is a Certified Human Resources Professional and a member of both the HRPAO and the Strategic Capability Network.

TALENTLINK